MW00612463

TO:

_____

FROM:

_____

DATE:

_____

Do not fear, for I am with you;

do not be afraid, for I am your God.

I will strengthen you; I will help you;

I will hold on to you with my righteous right hand.

~Isaiah 41:10~

_____

Don't worry about anything, but in everything,
through prayer and petition with thanksgiving,
present your requests to God.
~Philippians 4:6~

Rejoice always, pray constantly, give thanks in
everything; for this is God's will for you in Christ Jesus.
~1 Thessalonians 5:16–18~

Be strong and courageous; don't be terrified
or afraid of them. For the LORD your God is the one who
will go with you; he will not leave you or abandon you."
~Deuteronomy 31:6~

Let us run with endurance the race that lies
before us, keeping our eyes on Jesus,
the source and perfecter of our faith.
~Hebrews 12:1–2~

Take delight in the LORD, and he will
give you your heart's desires.
~Psalm 37:4~

"Love the Lord your God with all your heart,
with all your soul, and with all your mind."
~Matthew 22:37~

And be kind and compassionate to one another,
forgiving one another, just as God also forgave you in Christ.
~Ephesians 4:32~

For you are saved by grace through faith,
and this is not from yourselves; it is God's gift—
not from works, so that no one can boast.
~Ephesians 2:8–9~

I have been crucified with Christ,
and I no longer live, but Christ lives in me.
~Galatians 2:20~

For we are his workmanship, created in
Christ Jesus for good works, which God
prepared ahead of time for us to do.
~Ephesians 2:10~

The one who walks with the wise will become wise,
but a companion of fools will suffer harm.
~Proverbs 13:20~

"Haven't I commanded you: be strong and
courageous? Do not be afraid or discouraged,
for the LORD your God is with you wherever you go."
~Joshua 1:9~

Trust in the LORD forever, because in the LORD,
the LORD himself, is an everlasting rock!
~Isaiah 26:4~

Do nothing out of selfish ambition
or conceit, but in humility consider others
as more important than yourselves.
~Philippians 2:3~

Blessed is the one who endures trials, because
when he has stood the test he will receive the crown
of life that God has promised to those who love him.
~James 1:12~

Because of the LORD's faithful love we do not
perish, for his mercies never end. They are new
every morning; great is your faithfulness!
~Lamentations 3:22–23~

Therefore we do not give up. Even though
our outer person is being destroyed, our inner
person is being renewed day by day.
~2 Corinthians 4:16–18~

Do not be conformed to this age, but be transformed
by the renewing of your mind, so that you may discern
what is the good, pleasing, and perfect will of God.
~Romans 12:2~

Trust in the LORD with all your heart,
and do not rely on your own understanding.
~Proverbs 3:5~

For the word of God is living and effective and sharper than any double-edged sword, penetrating as far as the separation of soul and spirit, joints and marrow. It is able to judge the thoughts and intentions of the heart.
~Hebrews 4:12~

The Lord does not delay his promise, as some
understand delay, but is patient with you, not wanting
any to perish but all to come to repentance.
~2 Peter 3:9~

"The LORD your God is among you, a warrior who saves.
He will rejoice over you with gladness. He will be
quiet in his love. He will delight in you with singing."
~Zephaniah 3:17~

But I know that my Redeemer lives,
and at the end he will stand on the dust.
~Job 19:25~

"Come to me, all of you who are weary
and burdened, and I will give you rest."
~Matthew 11:28~

Don't worry about anything, but in everything,
through prayer and petition with thanksgiving,
present your requests to God.
~Philippians 4:6~

Rejoice always, pray constantly, give thanks in
everything; for this is God's will for you in Christ Jesus.
~1 Thessalonians 5:16–18~

Be strong and courageous; don't be terrified
or afraid of them. For the LORD your God is the one who
will go with you; he will not leave you or abandon you."
~Deuteronomy 31:6~

Let us run with endurance the race that lies
before us, keeping our eyes on Jesus,
the source and perfecter of our faith.
~Hebrews 12:1–2~

Take delight in the LORD, and he will
give you your heart's desires.
~Psalm 37:4~

"Love the Lord your God with all your heart,
with all your soul, and with all your mind."
~Matthew 22:37~

And be kind and compassionate to one another,
forgiving one another, just as God also forgave you in Christ.
~Ephesians 4:32~

For you are saved by grace through faith,
and this is not from yourselves; it is God's gift—
not from works, so that no one can boast.
~Ephesians 2:8–9~

I have been crucified with Christ,
and I no longer live, but Christ lives in me.
~Galatians 2:20~

For we are his workmanship, created in
Christ Jesus for good works, which God
prepared ahead of time for us to do.
~Ephesians 2:10~

The one who walks with the wise will become wise,
but a companion of fools will suffer harm.
~Proverbs 13:20~

_____

_____

_____

_____

_____

_____

_____

_____

_____

_____

_____

_____

_____

_____

"Haven't I commanded you: be strong and
courageous? Do not be afraid or discouraged,
for the LORD your God is with you wherever you go."
~Joshua 1:9~

_____

Trust in the LORD forever, because in the LORD,
the LORD himself, is an everlasting rock!
~Isaiah 26:4~

Do nothing out of selfish ambition
or conceit, but in humility consider others
as more important than yourselves.
~Philippians 2:3~

Blessed is the one who endures trials, because
when he has stood the test he will receive the crown
of life that God has promised to those who love him.
~James 1:12~

Because of the LORD's faithful love we do not perish, for his mercies never end. They are new every morning; great is your faithfulness!
~Lamentations 3:22–23~

Therefore we do not give up. Even though
our outer person is being destroyed, our inner
person is being renewed day by day.
~2 Corinthians 4:16~

Do not be conformed to this age, but be transformed
by the renewing of your mind, so that you may discern
what is the good, pleasing, and perfect will of God.
~Romans 12:2~

Trust in the LORD with all your heart,
and do not rely on your own understanding.
~Proverbs 3:5~

For the word of God is living and effective and sharper
than any double-edged sword, penetrating as far as the
separation of soul and spirit, joints and marrow. It is able
to judge the thoughts and intentions of the heart.
~Hebrews 4:12~

The Lord does not delay his promise, as some
understand delay, but is patient with you, not wanting
any to perish but all to come to repentance.
~2 Peter 3:9~

"The Lord your God is among you, a warrior who saves.
He will rejoice over you with gladness. He will be
quiet in his love. He will delight in you with singing."
~Zephaniah 3:17~

But I know that my Redeemer lives,
and at the end he will stand on the dust.
~Job 19:25~

"Come to me, all of you who are weary
and burdened, and I will give you rest."
~Matthew 11:28~

Don't worry about anything, but in everything,
through prayer and petition with thanksgiving,
present your requests to God.
~Philippians 4:6~

Rejoice always, pray constantly, give thanks in
everything; for this is God's will for you in Christ Jesus.
~1 Thessalonians 5:16–18~

Be strong and courageous; don't be terrified
or afraid of them. For the LORD your God is the one who
will go with you; he will not leave you or abandon you."
~Deuteronomy 31:6~

Let us run with endurance the race that lies
before us, keeping our eyes on Jesus,
the source and perfecter of our faith.
~Hebrews 12:1–2~

Take delight in the LORD, and he will
give you your heart's desires.
~Psalm 37:4~

"Love the Lord your God with all your heart,
with all your soul, and with all your mind."
~Matthew 22:37~

And be kind and compassionate to one another,
forgiving one another, just as God also forgave you in Christ.
~Ephesians 4:32~

For you are saved by grace through faith,
and this is not from yourselves; it is God's gift—
not from works, so that no one can boast.
~Ephesians 2:8–9~

I have been crucified with Christ,
and I no longer live, but Christ lives in me.
~Galatians 2:20~

For we are his workmanship, created in
Christ Jesus for good works, which God
prepared ahead of time for us to do.
~Ephesians 2:10~

The one who walks with the wise will become wise,
but a companion of fools will suffer harm.
~Proverbs 13:20~

"Haven't I commanded you: be strong and
courageous? Do not be afraid or discouraged,
for the Lord your God is with you wherever you go."
~Joshua 1:9~

Trust in the LORD forever, because in the LORD,
the LORD himself, is an everlasting rock!
~Isaiah 26:4~

Do nothing out of selfish ambition
or conceit, but in humility consider others
as more important than yourselves.
~Philippians 2:3~

Blessed is the one who endures trials, because
when he has stood the test he will receive the crown
of life that God has promised to those who love him.
~James 1:12~

Because of the LORD's faithful love we do not
perish, for his mercies never end. They are new
every morning; great is your faithfulness!
~Lamentations 3:22–23~

Therefore we do not give up. Even though
our outer person is being destroyed, our inner
person is being renewed day by day.
~2 Corinthians 4:16–18~

Do not be conformed to this age, but be transformed
by the renewing of your mind, so that you may discern
what is the good, pleasing, and perfect will of God.
~Romans 12:2~

Trust in the LORD with all your heart,
and do not rely on your own understanding.
~Proverbs 3:5~

For the word of God is living and effective and sharper
than any double-edged sword, penetrating as far as the
separation of soul and spirit, joints and marrow. It is able
to judge the thoughts and intentions of the heart.
~Hebrews 4:12~

The Lord does not delay his promise, as some
understand delay, but is patient with you, not wanting
any to perish but all to come to repentance.
~2 Peter 3:9~

"The Lord your God is among you, a warrior who saves.
He will rejoice over you with gladness. He will be
quiet in his love. He will delight in you with singing."
~Zephaniah 3:17~

But I know that my Redeemer lives,
and at the end he will stand on the dust.
~Job 19:25~

"Come to me, all of you who are weary
and burdened, and I will give you rest."
~Matthew 11:28~

Don't worry about anything, but in everything,
through prayer and petition with thanksgiving,
present your requests to God.
~Philippians 4:6~

Rejoice always, pray constantly, give thanks in
everything; for this is God's will for you in Christ Jesus.
~1 Thessalonians 5:16–18~

Be strong and courageous; don't be terrified
or afraid of them. For the LORD your God is the one who
will go with you; he will not leave you or abandon you."
~Deuteronomy 31:6~

Let us run with endurance the race that lies
before us, keeping our eyes on Jesus,
the source and perfecter of our faith.
~Hebrews 12:1–2~

Take delight in the LORD, and he will
give you your heart's desires.
~Psalm 37:4~

"Love the Lord your God with all your heart,
with all your soul, and with all your mind."
~Matthew 22:37~

And be kind and compassionate to one another,
forgiving one another, just as God also forgave you in Christ.
~Ephesians 4:32~

For you are saved by grace through faith,
and this is not from yourselves; it is God's gift—
not from works, so that no one can boast.
~Ephesians 2:8–9~

I have been crucified with Christ,
and I no longer live, but Christ lives in me.
~Galatians 2:20~

For we are his workmanship, created in
Christ Jesus for good works, which God
prepared ahead of time for us to do.
~Ephesians 2:10~

The one who walks with the wise will become wise,
but a companion of fools will suffer harm.
~Proverbs 13:20~

"Haven't I commanded you: be strong and
courageous? Do not be afraid or discouraged,
for the Lord your God is with you wherever you go."
~Joshua 1:9~

Trust in the LORD forever, because in the LORD,
the LORD himself, is an everlasting rock!
~Isaiah 26:4~

Do nothing out of selfish ambition
or conceit, but in humility consider others
as more important than yourselves.
~Philippians 2:3~

Blessed is the one who endures trials, because
when he has stood the test he will receive the crown
of life that God has promised to those who love him.
~James 1:12~

Because of the Lord's faithful love we do not
perish, for his mercies never end. They are new
every morning; great is your faithfulness!
~Lamentations 3:22–23~

Therefore we do not give up. Even though
our outer person is being destroyed, our inner
person is being renewed day by day.
~2 Corinthians 4:16~

Do not be conformed to this age, but be transformed
by the renewing of your mind, so that you may discern
what is the good, pleasing, and perfect will of God.
~Romans 12:2~

Trust in the LORD with all your heart,
and do not rely on your own understanding.
~Proverbs 3:5~

For the word of God is living and effective and sharper
than any double-edged sword, penetrating as far as the
separation of soul and spirit, joints and marrow. It is able
to judge the thoughts and intentions of the heart.
~Hebrews 4:12~

The Lord does not delay his promise, as some
understand delay, but is patient with you, not wanting
any to perish but all to come to repentance.
~2 Peter 3:9~